Welcome To My Obituary

(Things I am too scared to say aloud)

Written by,

L.M.D

GIVE IT A PRETTY COVER, AND THEY'LL

SOON FORGET IT'S A CASKET.

x

This is a dedication, not a letter.

I dedicate, not only this exposé but my entire life to pain.
For if there was no pain, we would never know pleasure.

I dedicate this book to grief.
For if there was no grief, we would never understand happiness.

I dedicate this book to hate.
For if we never felt hate, we would never experience love.

And I can say with absolute certainty,

that I love you.

xx

Hi.

When I was 5 years old I used to bite my fingernails when I got nervous or anxious, and as I grew older so did this coping mechanism. My heart would flutter as these emotions racked my body and so this small guise developed into a habit I still have not been able to kick for 16 years.

Whenever I know I make a mistake my instant reaction is to smile, it's subconscious and I believe I do it to try and conceal my error.

I laugh at jokes, even those I don't find particularly funny, because I hate making others feel awkward when all they wanted to do was make me smile; I feel like I owe them something.

I overthink every action I, or the people I know, make - though if I find myself judging or criticizing them I scold myself, because I haven't experienced what they have in life.

I take what news I hear on social media or read in magazines with a pinch of salt, as I think it's there for pleasure rather than accuracy.

I don't discriminate.
People are people, humans are humans.
No matter their race, looks, religion, culture, gender, sexual preference, or orientation.

I try to be the best person I can be, though this can be a struggle if I'm not in a good place mentally.

I attempt to display kindness with every breath, but I do have a temper - although this is usually directed at myself.

I don't trust easily, and because of this, I find I see people as muses for my art.

And although I do love easily, I don't let others love me so freely because I don't want to disappoint or rely on anyone.

I seek to live in a world where people are respected for their expressiveness rather than feared for it.

I reach for a world in which people take the time to understand one another, at least before we are separated within the divides of society.

This is me,

L.M.D

Table of contents

Pain

It's bad today, debilitating in fact.

But the sun is shining

and so,

I take my sweating palms,

wobbling knees

to the door - breathe in, breathe out

opening the barricade

that separates me from my safe place,

to a world of impossibilities.

I'm tired of playing it safe.

So,

let's smoke on this blunt 'till the air is filled with fumes and my lungs
cancer,

maybe it will dull the pain of what I'm trying to avoid

or maybe,

I'm not so lucky.

I'm confused;

so please

take my shaking hand,

sooth my rasping breath,

and guide me to other entities,

of multiple complexities,

where I belong,

and can live as my own worst enemy.

I'm a pedestrian in my own skin, so I write more realities in my head, than I will ever face in truth.

I don't have the motivation,

to feel all that I should.

The empty white lines call to me endlessly,

but I stare unabashed into the abyss.

Wishing my ego to soar to new heights,

permitting me to love carelessly and thoroughly.

 Paralysing my drying tears in their haste to hate,

as I beg with remorse,

for a deliverance to my lost will

and peace to my tormented soul.

He asked with innocent wondering,

Why do you torture yourself the way you do, what do you get from it?

I bit my tongue as I ladled the thought,

the same thing you get when you lie.

Validation, security, belonging.

I'm as normal as normal can be,

just lurking in the shadows is a not so friendly friend,

who's comfort I cannot escape,

which is ironically,

or sardonically,

a reprieve because at least I can be honest and open

with the beast anchoring my swaying personalities.

I find myself apologising

in times that don't even warrant

an apology

it seems I'm sorry

is all I can fathom

under the onslaught

of my racing mind

Who are you?

And why are you so scared to find out?

We are taught not to be too opinionated, to speak when spoken to, to cage our wildest ambitions. But I've tried the life of a domesticated mouth, and it's certainly not for (fucking) me.

I was so afraid of not being enough

for the people I cared most for

that I began to wither away;

slowly but surely.

Don't allow the richness of tomorrow to be dimmed,

by lamenting yesterday.

It wasn't poetic when you left, it hurt, like fucking hell.

It was something I swore I could never make beautiful,

even with words.

But it's late, I'm lonely and it's dark - so here I am, wallowing in the embers that were left,

as you packed the sun and took off.

And sometimes I wonder

what could have been

if I had the courage

to take the chances

I do

when I am half way down a bottle of vodka.

They say pain and pleasure come in a package,

and seeing how the pleasure was all yours,

the pain must be all mine.

Stuck between pushing myself to be the best I possibly can be, or to just live life by my nomadic spirit.

To be everything, or to be free.

And I fear this may be the biggest debate I ever face,

the one within myself.

I don't wear my heart on my sleeve and I tend to be stoic in terms of my emotions.

So, if you want to know what I am feeling, then you need to take a meaningful glance at my nails.

If they are short, chewed mercilessly, red and raw, then I am either anxious or excited about an upcoming event.

If they are healthy, glistening and manicured then I am either happy or suicidal.

And if you must know which of the two I am, then take a meaningful glance at my eyes; they will tell you all I fail to say.

How ironic,

that my deepest want,

is to not want anything

at all.

Most people have it wrong,

death is inevitable,

it's the living that is optional.

I promise,

I will not let your demise be romanticised,

I will not allow it to be corrupted,

by some backward sense of beauty.

I feel you're just a little like me and if you are don't worry if society sees
you as a failure,

don't fret it,

society just never took the time to understand us.

It hasn't been the easiest journey, but that's the beauty of life.

For every smile there will be a tear,

and for every laugh there will be despair.

You don't have to rely on anyone else to break your heart; you're more than capable.

You don't have to rely on anyone else to put you back together; you're more than capable.

I'm sorry for everything and anything I may have previously done,

even if it was in another life,

to cause you pain.

But the one thing I will never do,

is apologise for being human.

I penned letters of goodbye,

to those whom I thought,

deserved them,

and not a single one,

did I address to myself.

Grief

Laboured breathes,

chest heaving,

they say to keep my head up,

maintain eye contact,

but they are missing my plight,

I am concealed amongst heaped sorrows,

my own and accounts of others,

buried underneath the corpse of grief,

shallow exhalation,

with an almighty shove,

from under the dead weight,

I will rise.

I'll see you again, of that I am sure.

Even though we will end up in completely different homes,

I know I will see your glamorous smile once more.

For you fought long enough,

And now it is my turn.

All you will have to do is look down,

And me up.

Sometimes all I need is a shot of Tennessee.

Other times,

all I need

is for you

to pick up

on the other end.

I feel like I am living someone else's dream.

Someone who is a whole lot prettier,

has a wit as fast as their tongue,

has the smarts of Einstein,

a way with words

which would leave the likes of

Edgar Allen Poe envious,

someone who moves to their own beat,

with a rhythm as smooth as silk,

dancing all day and night,

until the wolves call her home

- each full moon.

It's troubling,

being troubled,

in a troublesome world.

I had you,

once, twice, thrice.

And still that wasn't enough.

I held you,

once, twice, thrice.

And still I begged for more.

You played me,

once, twice, thrice.

And still,

you laugh as I return.

I'm still waiting for the day I won't let the words I hold

closest to my heart burn a hole through it.

Though the warmth is welcome,

so maybe,

just faintly,

silently,

I don't mind it all that much.

I wish someone would have told me how hard it is

- how hard it can be -

to simply live, and if they had I wonder

who would I be now?

Less damaged (undoubtedly).

But possibly a dick (undoubtedly).

And I know I trigger myself sometimes,

I could lie and say

I don't do it on purpose,

though I do and honestly,

I know it's wrong,

but the darkness feels like home,

and it's really hard to leave home,

when it's all you have known,

but I also know that it's not quite

as impossible as it feels.

Just know that if we talk,

and I mean really talk

-

that our conversations venture into more important subtext than how the
weather faired that day

-

that you are special to me.

Because I don't *talk* with just anyone.

my mind is a labyrinth,

with twists and turns,

half the time,

I don't know if I am rising,

or sinking,

going left,

or going right,

but I'm okay,

because,

if you have no direction,

you can take any route,

and any route is progress,

right?

If I could dedicate my life to one thing,

I would to see to it

that no one ever goes through the grief the human mind can inflict upon you.

But as well as a dreamer, I am also a realist.

So, I will dedicate my life to letting you know,

that you are worthy and understood.

I put myself through grief for simply existing,

years later I am gratified

for allowing myself to simply live,

and to live simply.

I want to be worthy.

I want to finally be at ease with myself.

To feel deserving of the love others extend to me.

I want to be able to look people in the eye when I smile and not worry if they are criticising me.

I want to be able to grow with new forming relationships instead of detaching myself in fear of being hurt.

I want to feel these things,

I want to be deserving of these things,

because it has taken me too many years and too many internal struggles to be deserving of anything less.

People change. But the memories don't.

And as much as it may hurt to realise this,

there is also nothing quite so freeing.

Ever since you left I've had a hard time concentrating, staying focused. All my thoughts are one turn away from self-destruction. It feels like I will never be the same person I once was - and I'm not sure if that is a blessing in disguise, or tragic.

There's a secret I know,

about how water helps plants grow,

and that it's okay to cry,

you don't have to be so shy,

because there is no shame,

for wallowing in the rain.

You are:

The bravest of cowards,

The strongest of fighters.

Fuck it, let's go a little mental,

a little bat-shit crazy.

I show cowardice when I drink,

as I do it to escape.

But I am bravest when I pour that last shot,

because I know at the bottom,

that's where the memories lurk.

Returning me to my reality once again,

and making me fight through hell as I battle my demons,

with each blistering swallow;

It's what they call a catch-22

Perfection is an illusion,

based off one person's perspective,

and we're not all the same height;

So why do we allow others to dim our light?

Lust and love, such a fine line between the two.

My question is,

'How screwed are you, if you suffer from both afflictions?'

Others

stress

their

nostalgia

for

who

I

used

to

be

instead

of

cherishing

my season

of bloom

It is when I am at my happiest that I am most scared; as I am submerged in a flux of anxiety, waiting for my next descent.

And it is when I am at my worst that I am neutral; When I cannot feel anything at all.

Hate

How could you hate yourself so much?

When half of you is yet to be discovered.

Some people, for their battles,

take a needle to the vein,

others take shots of tequila.

I take the words aimed at me,

and fire back.

I will give you love,

when you have none left to give.

I will love you,

for those times you don't love yourself.

It's hard being different,

but I wouldn't change it for the world,

and neither should you

For so long I was hateful.

Hiding it behind a smile - I hate my smile.

Hiding it behind a laugh - I hate my laugh.

Hiding it behind a song - I hate my songs.

Lucky for me though,

I love smiling, laughing and music.

Made living a tad easier for a tad longer.

I hate the way you used me,

I hate the way I allowed it,

I hate the way I went back,

for a serving of

seconds, thirds and fourths.

I can't tell you the weight that was lifted from my shoulders when someone told me I didn't have to hate myself.

So, in the interest of the butterfly effect,

I am telling you this now.

And in the interest of humanity,

I dare you, no I double dare you,

to tell someone else.

I once made friends with a monster
that took residence in my creaky,
flood ridden,
roach infested,
attic of a mind.
It crept in on a cold and lonely night,
making itself at home
by soothing my overworked
and overtaxed head
with a velvet tone.
Easing my mind,
by distracting it from the insomnia
with beautifully woven words of hate.

Curing my one disease, by inflicting another

Nothing will kill you so easily and repeatedly,

as trying to outlive other's expectations of you.

The magic only happens,

when you out live your own.

Label the misfits,

those who are less fortunate,

restricted to walk when moonlit.

Those prone to more argument,

for what makes their heart skip a beat,

ostracized by their parliament.

Commence the quiet of the conceit,

we are only human though we don't accept,

and all we do is compete.

The mentality don't ask don't tell reject,

stands firm with lips shut and kept secrets,

there are injustices in the world held in neglect;

as we seen not normal face alienation for uniqueness.

Sometimes I wish someone would have told me,
or even hinted at the idea of a 'come down',
maybe then I would think more of myself than 'damaged goods'.

Do you ever wonder about us?

How maybe if we had of loved a bit harder,

we may still be together.

Or how maybe if we had of loved a bit harder,

We may have hated each other enough to love again.

Stars remind me of lost souls returning home.

Flying through, and burning up, the galaxy.

Awaiting to be claimed by someone once loved or scorned.

Hate is just the way-ward cousin of love,

whose parents didn't read them a story,

give them a kiss,

and tuck them in at night.

You get sad before you get angry,

anger only comes after embarrassment calls.

You get rejected before you get hurt,

hurt only comes after humiliation texts.

Both responses are caused by the people you love.

Suppose this means that love is our default.

And hate is just our armour.

come lay your head

deep in the expanse of my lap

close your eyes

as I run the fingers of my free hand

through your mop of hair

whilst my other cradles the back of a book

which houses the words I won't speak

instead I will whisper the sweet nothings

of my mind

in your ear

and with your eyes closed

you will never know

that you are the poet

of the poetry I write

with those fingers

of my free hand

combing through

all the things

you make me feel.

I wonder if there are people
whom like I
are addicted to their own misery

How odd, the insidiousness that nearly killed me was also the only thing that saved me from myself.

And how odd, that now it is gone I live this life in isolation, praying for its return.

'Love is stronger than death, isn't it?'

'Not if death is the result of love.'

And gradual changes,

somehow became,

gradual consumptions.

If you are so intent on taking things from me,

could you not at least take the bad parts.

They say if you lose something to retrace your steps.

So,

this time,

I'll start by hating you.

I've found over the years that it is these self-inflicted wounds I have endured, through my war, that are the hardest to overcome.

And I find it incumbent to mention that my internalised war was not silent. It was, by all means though a secret. Nevertheless, it was loud - deafening even.
In actuality, during those moments of despair, I was the loudest I had ever been.

Laughing through a clenched jaw,

applauding despite my shaking fists,

searching through crowds with evanescent eyes and,

maintaining fluent conversation despite the stutter of my sanity.

Just know if I ever say,

'asking for a friend'

I mean one of my multiple personalities.

I want to be one of those people;

with flowers in their hair,

who dance in fields of tall grass,

with sun bleached skin,

who smile over the smell of the ocean.

I want to be one of those people who are happy.

It's easier to write about hate, whilst thinking of love.

It's easier to write about love, whilst thinking of hate.

Riddle me this.

Love

To those I love,

I vow to never deprive you of your ambitions.

Truthfully all I want to do,

in an amongst all the

pain, anger and suffering,

is to worship you.

They always tell us about falling into love, but what about those times we step into it?

Those moments where we rationalise before taking the plunge, when we can say 'yes, this is what I want and here is why...' with a list of reasons so becoming the trees begin to bloom despite it being the middle of winter.

How about those moments where we voluntarily thrust ourselves into the affection instead of being at mercy to the impossibility of turning our backs?

Because we value the authenticity of love for its spontaneity, neglecting the wonder and amazement of its deliberateness.

Forgive me for my sins,

cleanse me of my transgressions,

absolve me of loving you.

What I would do to belong to someone,

who like I,

chose to belong to no-one.

Oh, what I wouldn't give.

I can deal with most things.

I can deal with

loss,

betrayal,

love,

pain,

envy,

angst,

shame,

embarrassment,

lies,

but I draw the line at you.

I fear I am incapable of love,

I don't suppose I hold the capacity of completely giving myself to another.

To have them see all the faults I consist of, and silently walk away; leaving my cries of mercy bouncing off the walls, echoing in the distance of yesterday's laughs.

I need you to choose me, against all other prospects,
all other worldly dramas, against all odds.

I need you to choose to want me

The

Odds

May

Be

Against

Us

But

I

Have

Never

Been

Good

With

Numbers

Your eyes held mine like the old fellow held the bottle

unwavering.

(And close to the heart)

The worst thing you could possibly do is fall in love with a poet.
You will be falling for their words, and they will make you feel everything,
but for only a ghost.

I watched, mesmerized at how dexterous your hands played the chords.

Flying from one string to the next so swiftly,
I could feel the gentle breeze from where I stood.

I swayed slightly, as a smile grew,
thinking the fiddler was different to how I imagined.

Until it was your turn to play me. You were not always so careful with heartstrings,
as you were with that of a violin.

I find solace in poetry,

it's the place where one comes to be reborn,

but never die.

All love is fabricated darling

so pull on that thread,

you don't want to be the only one

 to come undone.

What's my saddest story?

I've kissed boys.

I've kissed girls.

I've kissed people I have loved.

But I have never kissed anyone,

whilst being in love.

You scratched my heart,

just enough for it to sting with every breathe,

just not enough for it to heal itself,

and begin anew again.

It's not always so fake when I smile,

not anymore,

and that's my biggest flex.

A hallucinogenic trip

would be easier to undergo,

than deciphering the depth of my soul,

and its many contradictions.

I love with such ferocity,

it's misguided by the hands of hate,

however,

those loose hanging limbs are constructed of joy.

I have so much to say,

my voice trembles with a nervous tongue,

and maybe, quite possibly so,

that is why I feel a gust of guilt, when telling these truths,

to you.

She finally realised she had to stop living her life in the pursuit of others affections,

but rather,

to chase stars and live to make herself happy;

and that was when she found peace and certainty hiding within herself.

We're all just walking carcasses,
who make things more complicated than they need to be,
who over-think every minor aspect of our lives,
who grow too nervous over simple tasks
 and who forget to smile at the simple things.

We are nothing more than walking carcasses,
there is no need to be in the pursuit of anything other
than cadavers with the same stroll as ours.

Depression came by last week,

asked if I was glad I stayed around.

I replied curtly and with a sure nod of my head,

it asked who I was glad I stayed for.

I instantaneously responded 'Myself'.

And that is how I know for certain,

that I am over you.

It's time to be gentle with yourself, and to learn how to love yourself.

It's a cliché until it's not.

Until you realise how wonderful you can be.

Until you wake up and smile at the possibilities of today.

Until you meet adversity with sincerity.

Until you are able to find peace within fear.

Until you understand that life is worth living so it's time you start chasing after it.

Until you feel happiness whilst simply being.

It's a cliché until it's not;

then it is a cliché no more.

Lately I've been wondering,

painting wonderful pictures,

with the gentle stroke of my tongue,

on your mind - late at night,

how varied we are,

your vigorous need of competence,

my need of acceptance,

your dependency for all to conform,

my need to riot the forecast,

so lover,

I am not all that sorry,

that I'm in need of a thorough disconnection,

to express freely,

how it is the nocturnal,

starving artists,

who keep the world turning

I got so much love on the brain,

truthfully, it's a little painful.

I'm desperate for a love that feels like the first sip of freshly brewed coffee
on the morning of a winters day.

I'm in love with the way I remember you.

Completely, head over heels.

'How do you inspire the uninspired?'

'Simple, you care enough to listen.'

I think I'm now ready

to let myself be happy.

And when I'm on my death bed,
alone and cold,
shrivelled and frail,
it will all be okay,
so long as I have lived my life
in the pursuit of being kind.

xxx

This is a letter, not a dedication.

Thank you, for giving me a voice.

For laying down the foundations on which I am now able to stand upon
and speak the truths I would otherwise internalise.
Thank you for having the courage to stand up
under the invisible scrutinies of society
and bring me a peace I would have never otherwise understood
nor respected.

Thank you.

xxxx

Thank you for getting to know me.

Please leave a review and feel free to send me an email

l.m.d.poems@gmail.com

Follow me on Instagram, to stay up to date with my work

@l.m.d.poems

Printed in Great Britain
by Amazon